D0811790

JUVENILE

AUG

DANGEROUS PLANTS AND MUSHROOMS

The Encyclopedia of Danger

DANGEROUS ENVIRONMENTS

DANGEROUS FLORA

DANGEROUS INSECTS

DANGEROUS MAMMALS

DANGEROUS NATURAL PHENOMENA

DANGEROUS PLANTS AND MUSHROOMS

DANGEROUS PROFESSIONS

DANGEROUS REPTILIAN CREATURES

DANGEROUS SPORTS

DANGEROUS WATER CREATURES

CHELSEA HOUSE PUBLISHERS

The Encyclopedia of Danger

DANGEROUS PLANTS AND MUSHROOMS

Missy Allen

Michel Peissel

CHELSEA HOUSE PUBLISHERS

New York   Philadelphia

THE ENCYCLOPEDIA OF DANGER includes general information on treatment and prevention of injuries and illnesses. The publisher advises the reader to seek the advice of
medical professionals and not to use these volumes as a first-aid manual.

On the cover   Watercolor painting of henbane by Michel Peissel.

Chelsea House Publishers

Editor-in-Chief   Richard S. Papale
Managing Editor   Karyn Gullen Browne
Copy Chief   Philip Koslow
Picture Editor   Adrian G. Allen
Assistant Art Director   Howard Brotman
Manufacturing Director   Gerald Levine
Systems Manager   Lindsey Ottman

Encyclopedia of Danger
Editor   Karyn Gullen Browne

Staff for DANGEROUS PLANTS AND MUSHROOMS
Associate Editor   Terrance Dolan
Production Editor   Marie Claire Cebrián-Ume
Designer   Diana Blume

First Printing

1 3 5 7 9 8 6 4 2

Library of Congress Cataloging-in-Publication Data

Peissel, Michel
Dangerous plants and mushrooms/Michel Peissel, Missy Allen.
p. cm.—(The Encyclopedia of danger)
Includes bibliographical references and index.
Summary: Describes 24 dangerous mushrooms and other plants, from aconite
to water hemlock.
ISBN 0-7910-1787-7
1. Poisonous plants—Juvenile literature. 2. Mushrooms, Poisonous—Juvenile
literature. 3. Dangerous plants—Juvenile literature. [1. Mushrooms, Poisonous.
2. Poisonous plants. 3. Dangerous plants.] I. Allen, Missy. II. Title. III. Series:
Peissel, Michel. Encyclopedia of danger.
                                                                    91-44271
QK100.A1P45 1992   CIP
581.6'5—dc20   AC

CONTENTS

THE ENCYCLOPEDIA OF DANGER

"Mother Nature" is not always motherly; often, she behaves more like a wicked aunt than a nurturing parent. She can be unpredictable and mischievous—she can also be downright dangerous.

The word *danger* comes from the Latin *dominium*—"the right of ownership"—and Mother Nature guards her domain jealously indeed, using an ingenious array of weapons to punish trespassers. These weapons have been honed to a fatal perfection during millions of years of evolution, and they can be insidious or overwhelming, subtle or brutal. There are insects that spray toxic chemicals and insects that go on the march in armies a million strong; there are snakes that spit venom and snakes that smother the life from their victims; there are fish that inflict electric shocks and fish that can strip a victim to the bones; there are even trees that exude poisonous gases and flowers that give off a sweet—and murderous—perfume.

Many citizens of the modern, urban, or suburban world have lost touch with Mother Nature. This loss of contact is dangerous in itself; to ignore her is to invite her wrath. Every year, hundreds of children unknowingly provoke her anger by eating poisonous berries or sucking deadly leaves or roots; others foolishly cuddle toxic toads or step on venomous sea creatures. Naive travelers expose themselves to a host of unsuspected natural dangers, but you do not have to fly to a faraway country to encounter one of Mother Nature's sentinels; many of them can be found in your own apartment or backyard.

The various dangers featured in these pages range from the domestic to the exotic. They can be found throughout the world, from the deserts to the polar regions, from lakes and rivers to the depths of the oceans, from subterranean passages to high mountaintops, from rain forests to backyards, from barns to bathrooms. Which of these dangers is the most dangerous? We have prepared a short list of 10 of the most formidable weapons in Mother Nature's arsenal:

Grizzly bear.   Undoubtedly one of the most ferocious creatures on the planet, the grizzly needs little provocation to attack, maul, and maybe even eat a person. (There is something intrinsically more terrifying about an animal that will not only kill you but eat you—and not necessarily in that order—as well.) Incredibly strong, a grizzly can behead a moose with one swipe of its paw. Imagine what it could do to *you*.

Cape buffalo.   Considered by many big-game hunters to be the most evil-tempered animal in all of Africa, Cape buffalo bulls have been known to toss a gored body—perhaps the body of an unsuccessful big-game hunter—around from one pair of horns to another.

Weever fish.   The weever fish can inflict a sting so agonizing that victims stung on the finger have been known to cut off the finger in a desperate attempt to relieve the pain.

Estuarine crocodile.   This vile human-eater kills and devours an estimated 2,000 people annually.

Great white shark.   The infamous great white is a true sea monster. Survivors of great white shark attacks—and survivors are rare—usually face major surgery, for the great white's massive jaws inflict catastrophic wounds.

Army ants.   Called the "Genghis Khans of the insect world" by one entomologist, army ants can pick an elephant clean in a few days and routinely cause the evacuation of entire villages in Africa and South America.

Blue-ringed octopus.   This tentacled sea creature is often guilty of over-kill; it frequently injects into the wound of a single human victim enough venom to kill 10 people.

Black widow spider.   The female black widow, prowler of crawl spaces and outhouses, produces a venom that is 15 times as potent as rattlesnake poison.

Lorchel mushroom.   Never make a soup from these mushrooms—simply inhaling the fumes would kill you.

Scorpion.   Beware the sting of this nasty little arachnid, for in Mexico it kills 10 people for every 1 killed by poisonous snakes.

DANGEROUS PLANTS AND MUSHROOMS

Without plants, the Earth as we know it could not exist. Plants and plantlike fungi, or mushrooms, provide essential nutrition for all forms of life on this planet. Many of our most important medicines are derived from plants and mushrooms, and these life-forms even influence our spiritual existence and our ideals of art and beauty. Indeed, plants provide the very oxygen we breathe (through photosynthesis). Today more than ever before, as the rain forests shrink and the cities grow, the importance of plant life on Earth cannot be overemphasized.

Plants and mushrooms can also be dangerous, however. In 1974, according to the Food and Drug Administration, plants topped the list of poisonous substances swallowed by children. (In previous years, aspirin had been first on this list. The increased number of plant poisonings was related to the back-to-nature movement of the early to mid-1970s.) And in 1990, the American Association of Poison Control Centers reported that there were 63,000 cases of plant poisoning in the United States during that year alone. Some of these poisonings were the result of an occurrence that every parent is familiar with—a child innocently putting something dangerous in its mouth. Other poisonings were caused by adults using dangerous plants or mushrooms as food, as medicine, or for "recreational" purposes (as mood-altering or hallucinogenic substances). Still others were the result of inadvertent contact with a plant such as poison ivy. Almost all of these accidental poisonings could have been avoided, because the primary cause for most of them was simply a lack of education about plants and mushrooms.

Introduction

Because they lived in what was primarily an unsettled wilderness, our ancestors were much more familiar with plants and mushrooms than most of us are today. Native Americans were particularly well acquainted with North America's plant life; botany was an important part of their culture. Most contemporary Americans, on the other hand, can only recognize a handful of plants and flowers; we get our mushrooms at the supermarket and our plants and flowers from a florist. Modern urban and suburban life would not seem to demand a working knowledge of botany. But as this volume—and the 63,000 episodes of plant poisoning that occurred in 1990—will attest, even the most seemingly benign of houseplants or backyard mushrooms may have deadly potential. And education is the best method of prevention.

Prevention

- If you are planning to buy a plant, find out about the plant. Is it poisonous? Ask your florist or read up on the subject.
- Never put parts of *any* plant or mushroom in your mouth.
- Know what kind of plants grow in your yard or near your residence. Identify the dangerous ones.
- Pick and dispose of mushrooms growing on or near your property unless you can positively identify them as safe.
- Do not attempt to make herbal remedies.
- Avoid smoke from burning plants and leaves, which may carry plant toxins.
- Keep syrup of ipecac, which induces vomiting, on hand in case of an accidental ingestion of a poisonous plant or mushroom.

KEY

HABITAT

FOREST

SEA

WOOD/TRASH

TOWNS

SHORE

GRASS/FIELDS

MOUNTAINS

SWAMP/MARSH

GARDEN

FRESH WATER

JUNGLE

BUILDING

DESERT

CITIES

KEY

HOW IT GETS PEOPLE

INGESTION

TOUCH

STING

BITE

SPIT

SPRAY

MAUL

CLIMATIC ZONE

TEMPERATE

TROPICAL

ARCTIC

MORTALITY

ONE

TWO

THREE

FOUR

DANGEROUS PLANTS
AND MUSHROOMS

ACONITE

HOW IT GETS PEOPLE

Species: Aconitum napellus

HOW IT GETS PEOPLE

HABITAT

HABITAT

HABITAT

CLIMATIC ZONE

RATING

In Act V of William Shakespeare's *Romeo and Juliet*, a "life–weary" Romeo, intent on committing suicide, seeks out an apothecary and asks him for a "dram of poison." For "forty ducats," the apothecary sells Romeo some poison and advises him to put the substance "in any liquid" and then to "drink it off." The poison, he assures Romeo, is strong enough to kill him even if he had the strength of "twenty men." Romeo quaffs the deadly cocktail and soon after begins to feel the effects of the poison, crying out, "O true apothecary! Thy drugs are quick . . . "

Aconite

The poison Romeo uses to kill himself is aconitine, derived from a plant called aconite. It is one of the deadliest poisons known. The immediate effects of aconite poisoning on humans were described by the 16th-century botanist John Gerard: "Their lipps and tongue swell forthwith, their eyes hang out, their thighs are stiffe, and their wits are taken from them." Indeed, aconite is so potent that it has long been used as a military weapon: in ancient China, aconite was used to poison arrowheads, and in the late 19th century, Indian soldiers poisoned wells with aconite in an attempt to stop advancing British troops. Nepalese hill tribes still use aconite to make the notorious *Bikh* poisons.

Name/Description

One might expect a superdeadly poison to come from an ugly, gnarled stem or an unsightly, pockmarked bulb, but aconite, *Aconitum napellus*, also known as monkshood, wolfsbane, friar's cap, and *casque de fer*, is a rather showy, flowering plant, prized as a hardy and ornamental perennial by European and American gardeners. Aconite, as the Greek naturalist Theophrastus explained, "grows everywhere and not only at

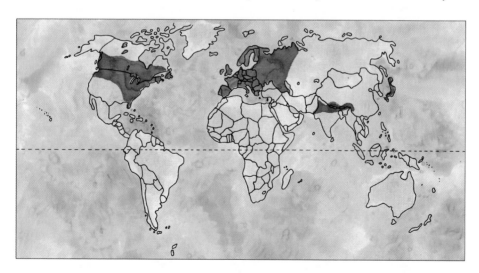

Akonai [Greece], from whence it gets its name." Usually about three feet tall, aconite produces helmet-shaped flowers, usually blue, but also white, pink, or off-white.

Accidental aconite poisonings are common; the dark-green, glistening leaves are a temptation and have occasionally found their way into a fatal salad. And the roots, the most toxic part of the plant, are often mistaken for horseradish. A small nibble will leave a person with a tingling tongue and a mild depression; a larger bite may prove to be a final one, for it only takes a milligram of aconitine to kill someone.

Pharmacology

Formerly used for treatment of heart disease, hypertension, sthenic (vigorous) fevers, and pulmonary infections, aconite is now considered to be of doubtful medicinal value, as safe doses are usually ineffective and larger doses are usually toxic.

Toxicology

All parts of the aconite plant are poisonous, especially the leaves and roots. The principal toxin is aconitine, and there are other poisonous alkaloids present as well. One milligram of aconitine can prove fatal, although it might take 10 milligrams to kill a large man.

Symptoms

Aconite ingestion will at first cause a sharp, burning sensation in the mouth, followed by a tingling and numbing of the throat—a sensation that soon spreads throughout the entire body. There will be nausea, vomiting, diarrhea, and abdominal pain. Later symptoms include chills, restlessness, staggering, dizziness, convulsions, constricted and then dilated pupils, impaired vision, low body temperature, irregular respiration, collapse, prostration, and coma. Death occurs from cardiac failure or respiratory paralysis.

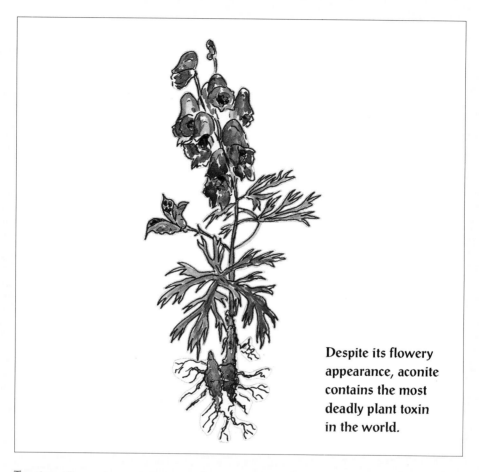

Despite its flowery appearance, aconite contains the most deadly plant toxin in the world.

Treatment

Evacuate the victim's stomach immediately. (Syrup of ipecac is an effective emetic, or vomit–inducing agent.) Atropine (see Belladonna) or digitalis (see Foxglove) may be administered to stimulate the heart and respiration. Inhalants such as ammonia, camphor, and sulfuric ether may be helpful, and artificial respiratory assistance may be required as well.

In extreme cases, ephedrine may be given intravenously.

AMANITA MUSHROOM

Genus: Amanita

HOW IT GETS PEOPLE

CLIMATIC ZONE

HABITAT

RATING

Mushrooms seem so terribly plain. For the most part, only mycologists (mushroom experts) and haute-cuisine gourmets seem able to raise much enthusiasm for these funny fungi. Most children loathe them. Eaten raw, they are about as exciting as oatmeal. Mushrooms do not even add color to a dish. But certain species—such as the *Amanita* mushrooms—have a rather exotic history, one that belies their run-of-the-mill reputation. It is a history that involves murder, mysticism, hallucinatory journeys, and even witchcraft.

In A.D. 54, Roman emperor Claudius I died after eating a dinner of *Amanita* mushrooms prepared for him by his wife, Agrippina, and her son, Nero. The deadly mushrooms got past the emperor's official taster, Halotus, because their poisons were slow working. By the time Halotus realized his mistake, it was too late for him and Claudius, and Nero became the new Roman emperor. (The treacherous Nero later had Agrippina killed, but she was beaten and stabbed to death rather than poisoned.)

Amanita Mushroom

One species of *Amanita*, known as fly agaric, is renowned for its psychotropic (affecting the mind) rather than its poisonous properties. The hallucinogenic effects of fly agaric seem to vary from person to person, but most takers have reported extravagant delirium and strange delusions. Some believed they could fly; others believed they were Jesus Christ. Fly agaric hallucinations are often interpreted in a religious context. The Koryak peoples of Siberia ingest fly agaric for spiritual and mystical guidance. So that none of the precious substance is wasted, the urine of an inebriated high-ranking Koryak is collected and then drunk by someone of lesser rank. Some historians believe that the Druids (the members of an ancient Celtic religious order) used fly agaric in their mystical ceremonies, and other historians believe that fly agaric played a role in the ecstasies of Old World witches' Sabbaths.

Name/Description

Amanita mushrooms are any of several species of white-spored, mostly poisonous fungi common to North America, Europe, and parts of Asia. The *Amanita* mushrooms have a prominent volva—a membranous sac or cup at the base of the stem. *Amanita* mushrooms are usually tall, with

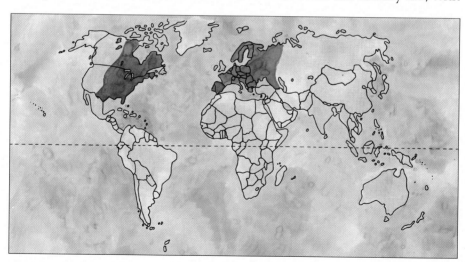

whitish stems and an umbrella-shaped, four- to six-inch diameter cap. They are usually found under or near deciduous (shedding leaves annually) and coniferous (cone-bearing) trees.

Toxicology

The principal toxins in fly agaric (*Amanita muscaria*) and the panther mushroom (*Amanita pantherina*) are ibotenic acid and muscimol, two closely related compounds. The death cap species (*Amanita phalloides*) and the destroying angel species (*Amanita virosa*) contain five toxins that cannot be removed by boiling or any other form of cooking.

Symptoms

Symptoms of fly agaric and panther mushroom poisoning develop within two hours of ingestion. They include dizziness, lack of coordination, muscle cramps and spasms, delusions, delirium, euphoria, and hallucinations. Symptoms of death cap and destroying angel poisoning develop more slowly and include severe abdominal pains, thirst, nausea, vomiting, and watery diarrhea. In extreme cases, a two-day remission may be followed by a recurrence of symptoms and then by jaundice, kidney failure, convulsions, coma, and death.

Treatment

For fly agaric and panther mushroom poisoning, administer activated charcoal in water, which will absorb the toxins. Other reactions should be treated symptomatically. Treatment for death cap and destroying angel poisoning must begin soon after ingestion. Vomiting should be induced, or gastric lavage (cleaning or purging of the digestive organs) should be administered at the nearest emergency room. Activated charcoal may be administered; later, glucose and penicillin may be helpful. Because of the destructive effect of *Amanita* toxins on the kidneys, a poisoning victim will remain subject to renal failure even after the toxins have been purged.

An infant was known to have been killed by Amanita poisoning simply through nursing.

Prevention

- Always follow the advice of mycologists Arne and Sally Benson: "The only way to know an edible mushroom from a poisonous mushroom is to know the species by name and by its history and reputation—when in doubt, throw it out."

BELLADONNA

HOW IT GETS PEOPLE

Species: Atropa belladonna

CLIMATIC ZONE

HABITAT

HABITAT

RATING

The dual nature of belladonna is apparent in its various names. In Italian, *bella donna* means "beautiful lady"; centuries ago, the *belle donne* of Venice used an extract of the plant to dilate the pupils of their eyes, which was considered to be a sign of beauty. But belladonna is also called deadly nightshade, devil's cherries, and devil's herb. According to old European legends, belladonna is the plant of the Devil, who tends to it with great care and unflagging devotion. And indeed, since pre–Christian times, belladonna has been employed for devilish purposes. Supposedly, belladonna was the plant that was used to poison the troops of the Roman general Marc Antony during the Parthian Wars in 36 B.C. And in his *History of Scotland*, the 16th-century Scottish writer George Buchanan recorded that under the reign of Duncan I, the soldiers of Macbeth poisoned a whole army of invading Danes by serving them, during a truce, a liquor spiked with belladonna.

Name/Description

Belladonna, *Atropa belladonna*, a coarse, branched herb of the nightshade family, is found in Europe, North Africa, North America, Russia, and India. Growing to about five feet high, it has reddish purple, bell-shaped flowers and shiny black berries. The belladonna root is a thick rhizome, or underground stem.

Pharmacology

Belladonna is one of the world's most important medicinal plants; it is essential in the treatment of eye diseases and is administered in almost

every ophthalmic operation. Atropine, the principal poisonous alkaloid in belladonna, has proven successful in the treatment of intestinal colic, nervous diarrhea, constipation, and urinal incontinence. Belladonna is also used as an antidote to opium.

Toxicology

The poisonous alkaloid atropine is present throughout the belladonna plant; its potency increases as the plant matures. The leaves and roots also contain other highly poisonous alkaloids. Most poisonings occur when children eat the berries.

Symptoms

Symptoms of belladonna poisoning include dryness of the skin, mouth, and throat, difficulty in swallowing, flushing of the face, cyanosis (bluish discoloration of the skin caused by insufficient oxygen), fever, rapid pulse, nausea and vomiting, dilation of the pupils, slurred speech, hysteria, hallucinations (mostly among children), convulsions, and delirium. Severe poisoning can lead to coma and death.

Treatment

Evacuate the stomach and the digestive tract. An injection of morphine may be given as an antidote.

Prevention

• Heed the advice of the naturalist Gerard: "Banish therefore these pernitious plants out of your gardens, and all places neere to your houses, where children or women with child do resort, which do oftentimes long and lust after . . . a berry of a bright shining blacke colour, and of such great beautie, as it were able to allure any such to eate thereof."

Three belladonna
berries are potent
enough to kill
a child.

BIG LAUGHING MUSHROOM

Species: Gymnopilus spectabilis

HOW IT GETS PEOPLE

CLIMATIC ZONE

HABITAT

HABITAT

HABITAT

RATING

The Japanese gave this mushroom its colorful name because, when ingested, it causes "unmotivated laughter and foolish behavior." A 20–year–old Japanese man who ingested these hallucinogenic mushrooms "became intoxicated and broke out in laughter. His hands and feet moved continuously as though he were dancing and he walked in zigzags like someone who had drunk too much sake [rice wine]." And the laughter and foolishness are not confined to Japan. In Ohio, a woman who nibbled on a big laughing mushroom reported experiencing "the most glorious visions of color and sounds of music."

Name/Description

The big laughing mushroom, *Gymnopilus spectabilis*, also known as the giant Gymnopilus and the showy flamecap (because of its bright orange cap), is found worldwide. Its colorful cap is two to six inches wide, with a fibrous surface. The stalk is solid and club–shaped and changes in color from orange or yellow to brown at its base. This mushroom has no distinctive odor and a very bitter taste. Big laughing mushrooms usually grow in clusters on or around trees and stumps.

Toxicology

Big laughing mushrooms contain large quantities of the hallucinogenic compound psilocybin.

Symptoms

The effects of psilocybin ingestion vary greatly and depend on the amount ingested, how the mushrooms were prepared, and the psychological and physical health of the individual in question. Within 30 minutes of ingestion, dizziness, giddiness, nausea, abdominal pain, muscle aches, shivering, anxiety, and restlessness may occur. These symptoms may be followed by visual and auditory disturbances and hallucinations, sweating, decreased concentration, lack of coordination, feelings of unreality, temporal distortions, delusions, difficulty in breathing, uncontrollable laughter, headache, and fatigue. In very severe cases of psilocybin poisoning, temporary paralysis has been reported.

Treatment

The individual should be kept calm and should be reassured that the symptoms are only temporary and will disappear in a few hours. In severe cases, tranquilizers may be administered. Alcohol is frequently consumed along with these mushrooms; its effects should be taken into consideration.

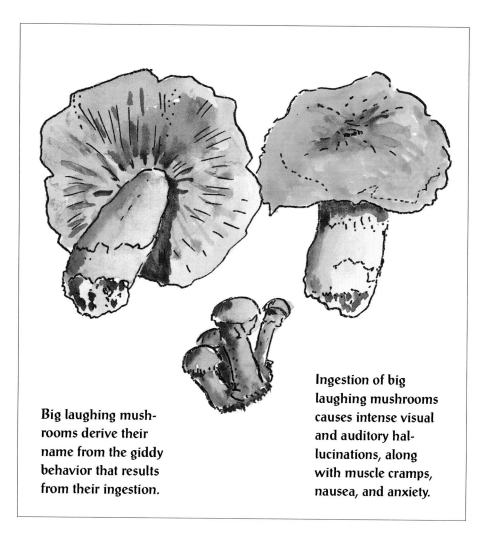

Big laughing mush-
rooms derive their
name from the giddy
behavior that results
from their ingestion.

Ingestion of big
laughing mushrooms
causes intense visual
and auditory hal-
lucinations, along
with muscle cramps,
nausea, and anxiety.

BITTERSWEET

HOW IT GETS PEOPLE

Species: Solanum dulcamara

RATING

HABITAT

HABITAT

HABITAT

CLIMATIC ZONE

CLIMATIC ZONE

For centuries, bittersweet has been used in herbal medicine. Its generic name, *Solanum*, is derived from the Latin *solari* (to console), and liquid extracts made from the boiled bark, roots, and shoots of bittersweet have been used for various medicinal purposes, including the treatment of rheumatism. According to the naturalist Gerard, bittersweet extract "is good for those that have fallen from high places, and have been thereby bruised or beaten, for it is thought to dissolve blood congealed or cluttered anywhere in the entrails and to heal the hurt places."

Bittersweet

The species name, *dulcamara*, means "bittersweet," and refers to the taste of the roots and stems, which, when chewed, are first bitter, then sweet. Sampling bittersweet is a bad idea, however, for it contains dangerous toxins. The majority of human poisonings occur when amateur naturalists make bittersweet "teas" for medicinal use and when children, attracted by bittersweet berries—which turn a bright scarlet red in the fall—suck on the berries and chew on the plant. Intrigued by the change of taste, children often gnaw on them for a long time, and because children are especially susceptible to the bittersweet's toxins, serious poisoning can occur.

Name/Description

Bittersweet, *Solanum dulcamara*, also known as bitter nightshade, woody nightshade, violet bloom, and scarlet berry, is found in temperate climates in North America, Europe, and Asia. It is a vinelike perennial with trailing or climbing stems up to 10 feet long and leaves that resemble those of the belladonna plant. Its star–shaped flowers, which bloom from April to September, are pinkish purple and hang in loose,

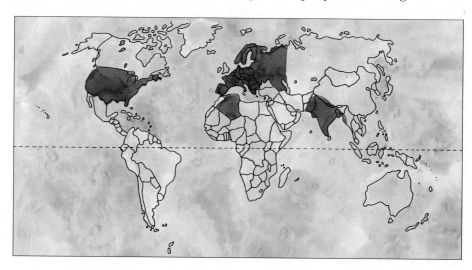

drooping clusters on short stalks opposite the leaves. Bittersweet berries are green at first, becoming orange and then bright red in the autumn; many remain on the plant long after the leaves have fallen.

Pharmacology

Over the centuries, bittersweet has been used as a treatment for rheumatism, as a narcotic, as a sedative, and, as Gerard noted, as a treatment for bruises, inflammations, and infections and skin diseases as well. Modern pharmacologists have learned that bittersweet extracts have antibiotic properties, and recent research also indicates that bittersweet contains a tumor-inhibiting agent that may someday prove effective in the treatment of cancer.

Toxicology

Bittersweet contains the alkaloid solanine, which has a narcotic effect on humans. In large doses, it can depress the central nervous system.

Symptoms

Bittersweet ingestion will be followed, after a period of several hours, by a burning sensation in the throat, nausea, vomiting, dilated pupils, diarrhea, weakness, slow respiration, dulled senses, low body temperature, dizziness, and delirium. There may also be irritation of the stomach and intestines, accompanied by abdominal pain. In severe cases, convulsions and even death may occur. Symptoms may persist for several days.

Treatment

Induce vomiting or administer gastric lavage. Subsequent dehydration should be corrected with fluid replacement (intravenously if necessary). Otherwise, treat symptomatically.

Poisonous bittersweet leaves come in the
deceptive shapes of hearts and flowers.

CHINABERRY

HOW IT GETS PEOPLE

Species: Melia azedarach

RATING

HABITAT

HABITAT

CLIMATIC ZONE

CLIMATIC ZONE

Throughout Asia, and much of Central and South America as well, different parts of the chinaberry tree have traditionally been used in a variety of ways. Its leaves are often utilized as insect repellents and as mothballs to protect woolens. Oils from the fruit of the chinaberry tree have been used in making candles, paints, soaps, and hair tonics. The pits of the fruits are fashioned into worry beads and rosary beads. Extracts from the chinaberry tree are also staple ingredients in regional folk remedies (see Pharmacology).

But the chinaberry tree is dangerous as well as useful. Children cannot resist playing with the wrinkled little berries; they make bracelets and necklaces from them and use them as ammunition for their pea shooters. Poisonings occur when children put the toxic chinaberries in their mouth. Although the bitter taste of the berries is usually enough to make a child spit them out immediately, sometimes they are swallowed, and children in Asia and South America have died after ingesting just a few. Poisonings also occur when overly potent medicinal "teas" are brewed from chinaberry leaves and then drunk as a cure for intestinal parasites.

Name/Description

The chinaberry tree, *Melia azedarach*, is found in Asia, South and Central America, Mexico, and the southern United States. It grows quickly but rarely surpasses 40 feet. The leaves are long and turn from light green to yellow in early winter, before dropping off. The chinaberry tree bears clusters of fragrant, delicate, white to purplish flowers, which have five or six petals. The fruit is a small, elongated, yellowish, wrinkled berry

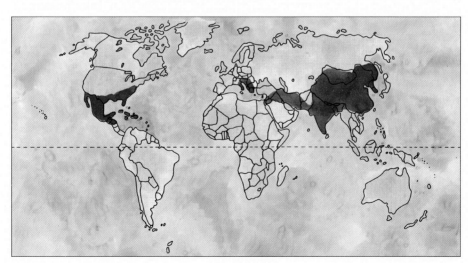

that remains on the tree after the leaves have fallen. When ripe, each fruit contains three to five smooth black seeds.

Pharmacology

Chinaberry tree extracts of one kind or another have been used to treat asthma, colds, cough, constipation, eczema, fever, headache, heat rash, hernia, leprosy and other skin diseases, rheumatism, ringworm, swellings, tumors, and ulcers. They have also been used to induce vomiting; to increase urinary output; to relieve pain and anxiety; and to induce sleep.

Toxicology

Saponin and other toxic substances that affect the central nervous system and the digestive tract are contained in the bark, leaves, flowers, roots, and fruit of the chinaberry tree. (The riper the fruit, the more toxic it is.)

Symptoms

Symptoms of chinaberry poisoning usually do not appear until several hours after ingestion. These symptoms include abdominal pain, vomiting, extreme thirst, diarrhea (often bloody), sweating, coldness of the extremities, weak pulse, confusion, stupor, labored respiration, convulsions, and in severe cases partial to complete paralysis, followed by death.

Treatment

If the victim has not vomited, induce vomiting or administer gastric lavage. Replace fluids to avoid dehydration. Otherwise, administer symptomatic care.

In parts of Asia and South America, chinaberries are used as mothballs, worry beads, hair tonics, and fish poison.

DATURA

HOW IT GETS PEOPLE

Genus: Datura

RATING

HABITAT

HABITAT

CLIMATIC ZONE

CLIMATIC ZONE

The narcotic and hallucinogenic properties of *Datura* plants have been known to various cultures around the world for centuries. *Datura* has traditionally been used as an intoxicant and an aphrodisiac; it has also played a role in the mystical and religious ceremonies of certain peoples. And perhaps more than any other psychotropic plant, *Datura* has been used in unsavory and sinister ways. In some countries, it has often been the chosen poison of assassins. Robbers have been known to put *Datura* seeds in drinks to stun potential victims, and burglars are said to blow pulverized *Datura* flowers and pollen through bedroom windows at night in order to drug the inhabitants, after which the house is ransacked.

Datura

The most notorious practitioners of criminal *Datura* use were the Thugs, a secret society of ritual murderers who preyed on unsuspecting travelers in India in the 18th and 19th centuries. The Thugs would fall in with a party of wayfarers, ingratiate themselves, and wait for an opportunity to drug their new friends with *Datura*. Once they were incapacitated, the victims would be strangled and offered up as a sacrifice to the Hindu goddess Kali. The Thugs would then rob the corpses of money or valuables before burying them.

Name/Description

Datura is the generic name for a number of species of widely distributed strong-scented herbs, shrubs, or trees of the nightshade family. In general, annual *Datura* shrubs grow to be four to five feet high, with smooth, downy leaves seven to eight inches long. The upturned, nearly erect flowers are usually white, yellow, or purple on the outside and white inside. The seed pod is about one and three-quarter inches wide, rounded, and covered with short spines. As the pod ripens, the stem

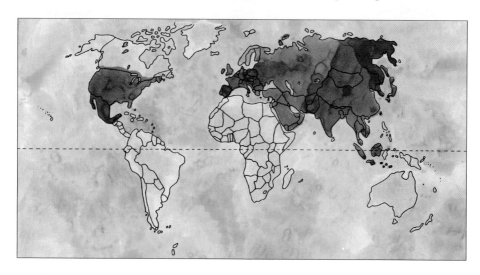

curves over so that the pod points downward, which enables it to split open and release the flat, brown, sweet-tasting seeds.

Pharmacology

Datura has been used for various medicinal purposes over the centuries. *Datura* cigarettes, for example, have been used as a treatment for bronchial asthma. Today, *Datura* is cultivated for the pharmaceutical industry in the United States, Europe, and Asia.

Toxicology

Datura contains atropine (also known as daturine)—which is also found in belladonna—and other hallucinogenic and toxic alkaloids, including scopolamine. The entire plant is toxic, including the nectar, but the seeds are most often implicated in poisonings.

Symptoms

Symptoms of *Datura* poisoning include a dry mouth, dilated pupils, dry, warm skin (occasionally with a reddening of the face and neck), rapid heart rate, and delirium with hallucinations. Later, there will be drowsiness, general weakness, high body temperature, lack of coordination, deep sleep, and in extreme cases, muscular and respiratory paralysis and death.

Treatment

Administer prompt gastric lavage. Treat convulsions with sedatives or anticonvulsants. If poisoning is severe, administer physostigmine

**Many children have been poisoned by simply
putting the Datura flower to their lips.**

intravenously. If the victim's temperature is very high, cool the body externally (by sponging). Moderate poisoning usually wears off in less than a day, but the victim may remain in a state of confusion for several days.

DUMBCANE

HOW IT GETS PEOPLE

Genus: Dieffenbachia

HOW IT GETS PEOPLE

HABITAT

HABITAT

HABITAT

CLIMATIC ZONE

CLIMATIC ZONE

RATING

What image does the average American doctor's office bring to mind? Plastic sofas, a No Smoking sign, thumb–worn magazines, and in one corner of the room, in an oversized flower pot, the ubiquitous, drooping *Dieffenbachia*. The *Dieffenbachia* is also known as the dumbcane plant. A patient nervously nibbling one of its leaves while he or she waited to see the doctor would soon realize how the dumbcane got its name, for the toxic leaves of this plant can literally render a person speechless.

Dumbcane

The toxic properties of the dumbcane plant have been known for centuries by South American Indians, who used dumbcane sap as a poison for arrows and spears and also as a means to sterilize their enemies. (Dumbcane extract was also used in sterilization experiments carried out by the Nazis in concentration camps during World War II.) Dumbcane does not have to be ingested to affect someone; dumbcane cuttings are known to root easily and quickly, and many victims suffer inflammation of the hands, wrists, and arms after chopping dumbcane stems into pieces in order to start new plants. And once it is on the hands, the toxin is easily spread to the mouth and eyes, causing swelling and irritation.

The most common victims of dumbcane poisoning are children. Dumbcane is the second most popular house and office plant (philo–dendron is first), and children frequently come into contact with it, often using it as play food. A doctor in Fort Pierce, Florida, reported that he treated one child for dumbcane poisoning twice in the same day. The second incident occurred when the boy used a pair of pliers to squeeze juice from the plant's stem!

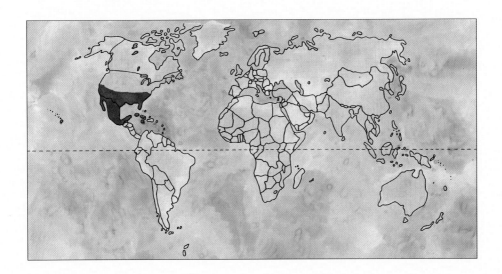

Name/Description

Dumbcane is any of 30 species of *Dieffenbachia*, a tropical, shrublike evergreen found in parts of North, Central, and South America. Dumbcane can grow to a height of eight feet. It has a thick, fleshy, succulent stem and green, oval leaves with whitish markings. Dumbcane has small flowers and small, round, bright-red fruit.

Toxicology

All parts of the dumbcane contain a toxin that, when ingested, causes inflammation of the pharynx and larynx, impaired speech, and, in extreme cases, death by suffocation.

Symptoms

Chewing on the plant produces an immediate and intense pain in the mouth, followed by swelling, burning, and blistering in the mouth and throat; nausea; abdominal pain; cramping; and diarrhea. Speech may become unintelligible. Contact with the plant's sap can cause irritation of the fingers, hands, wrists, arms, lips, and eyes.

Treatment

For swelling and pain inside the mouth, cool liquids and demulcents (substances that have a soothing effect on inflamed mucous membranes) held in the mouth may bring some relief. Analgesics may be given for pain. For skin poisoning, the affected area should be immediately and thoroughly cleaned, and a soothing lotion should be applied.

When ingested, the toxic leaves of the dumbcane plant render their victims speechless.

Ingestion of dumbcane is the second most common cause of plant poisoning among American children.

ERGOT

HOW IT GETS PEOPLE

Species: Claviceps purpurea

HABITAT

CLIMATIC ZONE

RATING

During the Middle Ages, the period of European history from about A.D. 500 to 1500, tens of thousands of Europeans were afflicted with a strange condition known as St. Anthony's fire. Racked with violent seizures, victims would scream and babble madly, claiming that they were being attacked by invisible monsters and demons and that their feet and hands were on fire. And indeed, their feet and hands would soon turn black, as though charred by flames, and pieces of "burned" flesh would fall off. During these epidemics, it was widely believed that the victims had been possessed by demons. Many of those who were afflicted by "the fire" prayed to St. Anthony or made pilgrimages to the saint's shrine in Egypt, for it was believed that he had special powers for the casting out of demons. But physicians, rather than saints, finally exorcized St. Anthony's fire. At the end of the 16th century, French physicians learned that St. Anthony's fire was caused not by demons but by "our daily bread," or more specifically, by ergot, a fungus that infected the rye from which the daily bread was made. The symptoms of St. Anthony's fire were actually the symptoms of ergot poisoning.

Name/Description

Ergot, which means "cock's spur" in French—the French physicians who discovered the fungus thought that the swollen rye grain on which it was found resembled a rooster's hind claw—is a lower species of fungus known as *Claviceps purpurea*. Ergot infects rye, wheat, barley, and other cultivated cereals, as well as some wild grasses, and is found in Europe, throughout the Caribbean, and in North America. (Some historians believe that ergot poisoning played a role in the witchcraft hysteria that struck Salem, Massachusetts, in 1699.)

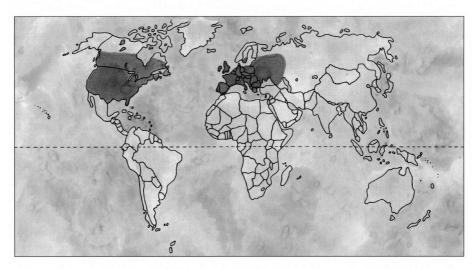

Pharmacology

Only the ergot that grows on rye is acceptable for pharmaceutical purposes. The ergot extract ergonovine stimulates the smooth muscles of the uterus and is used to bring about strong, rhythmic contractions during childbirth. Another extract, called ergotoxine, prevents excessive bleeding and has been used effectively to prevent or stop hemorrhaging during childbirth. Small amounts of the extract ergotamine are sometimes used to treat migraine headaches. Ergot also produces lysergic acid, which is used in the making of the powerful hallucinogen lysergic acid diethylamide, or LSD.

Toxicology

Ergot poisoning occurs when humans eat bread baked from flour made from ergot–infested grain. The principal toxic element is ergotoxine. Symptoms of ergot poisoning include gangrene and associated pains in the extremities, changes in blood pressure, chest pains, headache, breathing difficulties, vomiting, stomach cramps, slowed pulse, delusions, hallucinations, convulsions, and coma. Ergot poisoning may cause pregnant women to miscarry.

Treatment

Induce vomiting or administer gastric lavage. After the victim has vomited, administer activated charcoal to absorb the remaining toxins. Analgesics should be given for pain. Respiratory assistance may be required. An anticonvulsant should suppress seizures.

The hands and feet of ergot poisoning victims often turn black, as if charred by fire.

Eating bread made with ergot-tainted flour can be lethal.

FOXGLOVE

HOW IT GETS PEOPLE

Species: Digitalis purpurea

CLIMATIC ZONE

HABITAT

HABITAT

HABITAT

RATING

One of the great events in the history of botanical medicine was the discovery of the effects of foxglove extract on the human heart. How–ever, nobody knows exactly when this event took place or who was involved. The French claim that the discovery was made by a French physician in the 19th century; the British assert that it was made by Englishman Dr. William Withering in the 18th century. (In fact, both men were introduced to the curative uses of foxglove by country people who were well versed in folk medicine.) But nobody disputes the almost miraculous effectiveness of foxglove in the treatment of congestive heart failure. Nor does anyone dispute the potential danger of foxglove.

Foxglove

Digitalis, the foxglove derivative used in the treatment of cardiac ailments, contains powerful toxins. A little digitalis can avert congestive heart failure in a dangerously ill patient; a little more can kill that same patient by stopping the heart altogether. Dr. Withering visited a man in Yorkshire who had suffered a digitalis overdose when his wife made him an extra–strong foxglove tea. "This good woman knew the medicine of her country," Withering wrote, "but not the dose of it, for her husband narrowly escaped with his life."

Name/Description

Foxglove is just one of the many strange names given to this common, tall, but short–lived herb found in North America and Europe. Its species name is *Digitalis purpurea*. The popular term *foxglove* seems to have come from old European rural legends about the plant. According to these stories, fairies used the drooping, bell–shaped, purple blossoms as gloves (among other things). The peasants referred to the fairies as the "wee folk," the "good folk," or simply "the folk"; and thus the *Digitalis* plants

51

were "folk's gloves," which eventually became the term *foxglove*. According to a northern European legend, however, the term *foxglove* came about because mischievous fairies often gave *Digitalis* blossoms to foxes, who used them as gloves to keep their paws silent when they raided chicken coops. In France, foxglove is more reverently known as *gants de Notre Dame* (gloves of Our Lady) and *doigts de la Vierge* (Virgin's fingers).

Pharmacology

The principal medicinal use of the foxglove extract digitalis is as a heart stimulant in cases of congestive heart failure. Digitalis has also been effective in the treatment of diseases unrelated to the heart, such as glaucoma and muscular dystrophy. Digitalis is the antidote for aconite poisoning (see Aconite), and it is also an effective diuretic (a substance that increases urine output).

Toxicology

The entire foxglove plant is poisonous; the primary toxic substance is digitoxin, and there are other potentially poisonous substances in the plant as well. In adults, poisonings usually occur as a result of an accidental medicinal overdose. In children, poisonings occur when victims unknowingly eat or suck on the flowers, leaves, or seeds.

Symptoms

Symptoms of digitalis poisoning include dizziness, vomiting, irregular heart rate, severe headache, diarrhea, fatigue, and drowsiness. In acute cases of poisoning, victims experience visual disturbances, hallucinations, tremors, and delirium. Digitalis poisoning can be fatal.

When eaten, two to four foxglove leaves are potent enough to kill an adult human.

Treatment

Induce vomiting (if it has not already occurred) or administer gastric lavage. Administer atropine for cardiac complications.

HENBANE

HOW IT GETS PEOPLE

Species: Hyoscyamus niger

HABITAT

CLIMATIC ZONE

RATING

How potent are the hallucinogenic substances contained in the seeds of henbane? In *The Book of Poisons*, Gustav Schenk described the results of his own attempt to answer this question. After inhaling the fumes of roasting henbane seeds, Schenk reported that "My limbs lost their certainty, pains hammered in my head, and I began to feel extremely giddy. . . . I had the feeling that my head had increased in size; it seemed to have grown broader, more solid, heavier. . . . My heart was beating loudly. I didn't hear it with my ears, for they seemed to be deaf. . . . The room dances; the floor, the walls and the ceiling tilt slowly to the right and then back to the left. . . . Everything suddenly amused me. . . . I was seized by a raging impulse to move. Since my feet seemed firmly welded to the floor, I could only clutch and grasp at things with my hands and tear them to pieces. . . . There were animals, which looked at me keenly with contorted grimaces and staring, terrified eyes; there were flying stones and clouds of mist. . . . I was flung into a flaring drunkenness, a witches' caldron of madness."

Name/Description

Henbane, *Hyoscyamus niger*, is the most unsightly member of the night-shade family. Common to Europe, Asia, and North America, henbane has been likened to "a disease rendered visible." Its funnel-shaped flowers are an unpleasant greenish yellow color, and the entire plant is covered with long hairs that secrete a sticky, smelly substance. As if it were ashamed of its appearance, henbane can usually be found around rubbish piles, garbage dumps, and dung heaps.

Pharmacology

Despite its unappealing appearance, henbane has had a long and pro-ductive medicinal history. The ancient Assyrians used henbane as a

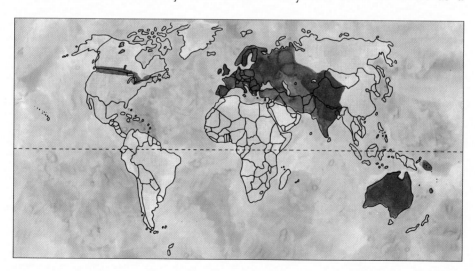

remedy for toothache. The Greek physician Dioscorides was familiar with its painkilling and sleep-inducing properties, and the Roman scholar Pliny the Elder recommended it for treating "toothache, gout, swelling, certain female troubles, and coughs." Today's physicians have also put this ugly plant to good use, primarily as a sedative and, in combination with other drugs, as an anesthetic for women in labor.

Toxicology

Pliny the Elder was well versed in the positive attributes of henbane, but he was aware of its negative side as well, warning that ingestion of the plant might cause "insanity and giddiness" (as Gustav Schenk could have testified). Ingestion of henbane can also cause death. All parts of the plant are poisonous, but the tiny seeds are responsible for most fatalities. Twenty seeds are enough to kill an adult. Henbane's principal toxins are hyoscyamine, hyoscine, and atropine.

Symptoms

Symptoms of henbane poisoning include dryness of the skin, mouth, and throat; bluish discoloration of the skin; headache; nausea and vomiting; slurred speech; blurred vision; excitement; delirium; hallucinations (mostly in children); and, in severe poisonings, stupor, convulsions, coma, respiratory failure, and death.

Treatment

Administer gastric lavage and a slow intravenous infusion of physostigmine. Sedatives or anticonvulsants may be necessary. Pilocarpine drops will reduce any eye discomfort.

Twenty tiny henbane
seeds can prove lethal
to an adult.

INKY CAP

HOW IT GETS PEOPLE

Species: Coprinus
atramentarius

CLIMATIC ZONE

HABITAT

HABITAT

HABITAT

HABITAT

RATING

Inky cap mushrooms are said to have an excellent, rather delicate taste. But diners who plan to round off an inky cap meal with a bottle of good wine—or any alcohol, for that matter—may find themselves in no condition to eat dessert. Inky caps are safe if they are eaten by a teetotaler, but in combination with alcohol they become toxic and produce peculiar and harrowing symptoms. Even if alcohol is ingested

58

three days after the inky caps were eaten, poisoning can occur. Recently, it was determined that the chemical makeup of inky cap mushrooms is identical to that of Antabuse, a drug developed in Sweden to treat alcoholics. People on Antabuse become violently ill if they drink alcohol, in much the same way as people who mix alcohol and inky cap mushrooms. Fittingly, the inky cap mushroom is also known as tippler's bane.

Name/Description

The name *inky cap* refers to the self–digestion process *Coprinus atramentarius* undergoes when it reaches maturity. During this process, the mushroom's gills (the plates that form the undersurface of the cap) liquify into a black, inky substance that releases ripe black spores. The fleshy, grayish cap itself is two to four inches wide, bell–shaped, and striated. Growing up to eight inches tall, inky caps are found in clusters in the spring and fall, on the ground or growing on rotten wood.

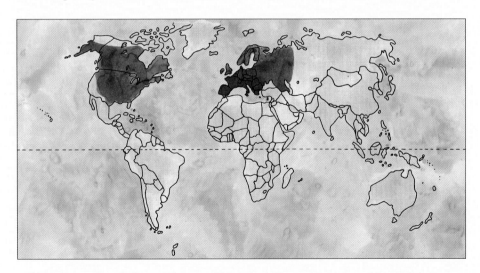

Toxicology

Inky caps contain coprine, a compound that reacts with alcohol in the human body to produce a poisonous substance, acetaldehyde.

Symptoms

Symptoms of inky cap poisoning vary, depending on the amount of mushrooms eaten, the quantity of alcohol drunk, and the interval between. Initial symptoms include discoloration of the face, neck, and sometimes the entire body; headache; a throbbing distension of the neck veins; a metallic taste in the mouth; chest pains; nausea; and sweating. In severe cases the tongue may become so swollen that it becomes difficult for the victim to breathe, and there may be visual disturbances, vertigo, weakness, confusion, and hypotension (abnormally low blood pressure). Fortunately, these symptoms are temporary and usually disappear as the alcohol level in the body diminishes.

Treatment

There is no known antidote for inky cap poisoning; treat symptomatically. Recovery is usually spontaneous and complete.

Prevention

• Avoid alcohol before, during, and after a meal that includes inky caps and for at least five days following the meal.

If ingested along with alcohol, inky
cap mushrooms can be toxic.

JIMSONWEED

HOW IT GETS PEOPLE

Species: Datura stramonium

RATING

HABITAT

HABITAT

HABITAT

HABITAT

CLIMATIC ZONE

CLIMATIC ZONE

In 1696 a colonist named Nathaniel Bacon led an uprising of Virginia frontier farmers against the local, British–backed government. During the rebellion, Bacon and his men burned the village of Jamestown to the ground. In the weeks that followed, many of the British soldiers who had been sent to Jamestown to put down the uprising, as well as many of the local citizens, found themselves facing starvation. Foraging in the countryside for edible vegetation, they made the mistake of ingesting jimsonweed, which resulted in one of the most bizarre scenes in American history. It was, wrote historian Robert Beverly, "a very pleasant comedy; for they turned natural Fools for several days [and] in this frantic condition they were confined, lest they in their Folly should destroy themselves." The incident supplied *Datura stramonium* with its common name—jimsonweed, or Jamestown weed.

A similar—but far less "pleasant"—incident occurred on a rural Tennessee farm in 1963. After eating lunch on an autumn afternoon, five people were beset by strange symptoms. By the time the five had been admitted to a local hospital later that day, they were experiencing severe nausea and spasms, delirium, and even hallucinations, including visions of swarms of insects and beautiful flowers. The local pathologist had something of a mystery on his hands. What had happened to these people? At first he suspected food poisoning, but then one of the farmers mentioned the tomatoes they had eaten for lunch, which had been grown in "a new way" by his brother-in-law. In order to make the tomato plants survive the fall frosts, he had grafted them to a local weed that usually grew tall and strong despite the cold weather. The

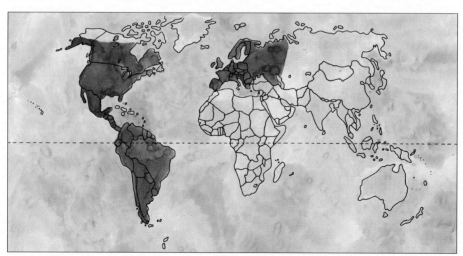

pathologist soon learned that this hardy, scraggly growth was jimsonweed, and the mystery was solved. (All of the poisoning victims recovered.)

Name/Description

Jimsonweed, *Datura stramonium*, also commonly known as thorn apple, is a tall (as high as five feet), thick–stemmed, coarse, evil–smelling member of the nightshade family. This disreputable weed is found throughout North America, usually along railroad tracks and highways and in barren fields, empty lots, and landfills. Jimsonweed has large, pointed leaves; white or pale violet trumpet–shaped flowers; and egg–shaped fruit covered with prickly thorns.

Pharmacology

The narcotic and hallucinogenic properties of jimsonweed may not have been known to the early American colonists or the British (before the Jamestown incident, that is), but since prehistoric times Native American peoples have used potions made from jimsonweed as anesthetics and sedatives and also to induce visions during religious ceremonies. Shamans, or tribal priests, were well acquainted with the potential toxicity of jimsonweed and they carefully regulated dosages. Today the jimsonweed extract stramonium is used in the treatment of asthma and other bronchial ailments.

Toxicology

All parts of the plant are poisonous. The primary toxic and hallucinogenic alkaloids are scopolamine, hyoscyamine, and atropine.

Symptoms

Symptoms of jimsonweed poisoning include headache, fever, nausea, vomiting, dizziness, thirst, a dry and burning sensation in the skin, pupil

Soup accidentally laced with jimson-weed seeds poisoned a California family.

dilation, confusion, hallucinations, and mania. In severe poisonings, convulsions and coma will be followed by death.

Treatment

Induce vomiting or administer gastric lavage. If necessary, sedate the patient. Reduce elevated body temperature by sponging with cool water. Pilocarpine may be given for dry mouth and visual disturbances.

LILY OF THE VALLEY

HOW IT GETS PEOPLE

Species: Convallaria majalis

CLIMATIC ZONE

HABITAT

HABITAT

RATING

Lily of the valley has long been associated with things sweet and pretty. Its perfumed, delicate, bell-shaped blossoms are a traditional favorite in bridal bouquets. The fragrant oil from the flowers is used in the making of perfumes and other toiletries, and the dried blossoms are frequently mixed with lilac, lavender, and violets in sachets, which were once known as sweet bags. In Europe, lily of the valley is a symbol of the Virgin Mary and is known as Our Lady's tears. Medieval monks, referring to the even, stairlike arrangement of flowers along the stem, called the plant ladder-to-heaven, or Jacob's ladder.

According to a medieval legend, the thick carpet of lilies of the valley in St. Leonard's Forest in Sussex, England, marks the places where good St. Leonard shed blood in an epic battle with a dragon. In the 15th century, water or wine in which lily of the valley was steeped was called *aqua aurea*, or golden water, and was kept in gold and silver vessels. But modern-day versions of golden water are to blame for many of the deaths associated with this nominally benign plant. Children have been known to drink the water that freshly cut lilies of the valley are often placed in. Because of the highly toxic substances contained in the plant, this playful mistake results in sickness and, in some cases, death.

Name/Description

Lily of the valley, *Convallaria majalis*, is a small, fragrant, perennial herb that grows from a slender, creeping rootstock, or rhizome. Waxy, white, nodding, bell-shaped flowers bloom in the spring on a single 4-to-10-inch upright stalk. Lily of the valley fruit ripens into bright orange-red, fleshy berries about a half inch in diameter.

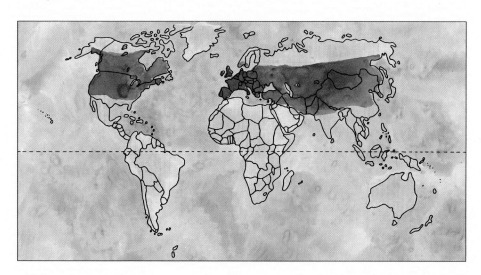

Pharmacology

As early as the 15th century, lily of the valley extracts were used medicinally. In the medieval guide to botany, *Hortus Sanitatis* (Garden of Health), they were recommended for the prevention of stroke and for the relief of gout, and it was also said that a certain lily of the valley extract rubbed on the neck and forehead would provide "good common sense." Today's physicians use digitalis–like substances derived from lily of the valley in the treatment of heart disease (see Foxglove).

Toxicology

The entire lily of the valley plant is poisonous. The two primary toxins are convallarin and convallamarin.

Symptoms

Symptoms of lily of the valley poisoning include pain in the mouth area, nausea, vomiting, abdominal pain, cramping, increased urination, and diarrhea. A severe poisoning may cause mental disturbances, cardiac irregularities, convulsions, and perhaps death.

Treatment

Induce vomiting or administer gastric lavage. Activated charcoal may be given to absorb the poison.

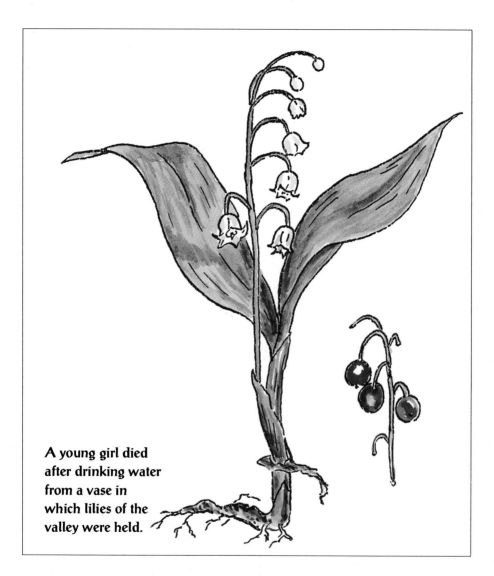

A young girl died
after drinking water
from a vase in
which lilies of the
valley were held.

LORCHEL MUSHROOM

Species: *Gyromitra esculenta*

HOW IT GETS PEOPLE

CLIMATIC ZONE

HABITAT

HABITAT

HABITAT

RATING

Lorchel mushrooms are truly odd–looking fungi. Their wrinkled, gnarled, scrunched–up caps have been described as looking like "knobby brains" and have earned the lorchels various descriptive nicknames, including elephant ears and brain mushrooms. In European markets, however, lorchels were given the species name *esculenta*, which means

70

edible. Despite their appearance, lorchels were, and still are, greatly sought after by mushroom connoisseurs; properly prepared, they are said to have a very pleasant flavor. Improperly prepared lorchels, on the other hand, make for a dangerous dinner. People have been known to become ill simply from inhaling the fumes from a boiling pot of lorchels. Eating raw lorchels can be fatal.

Name/Description

Gyromitra esculenta, also known as the lorchel or the false morel, is a medium-sized mushroom—three to seven inches tall—usually found during spring and fall in coniferous woodlands in North America and northern Europe. It often grows on rotting wood. The lorchel's cap is hollow and saddle-shaped, brown on top and white underneath. The hollow stem is pinkish white. The lorchel has thin, waxlike flesh and a mild, agreeable odor.

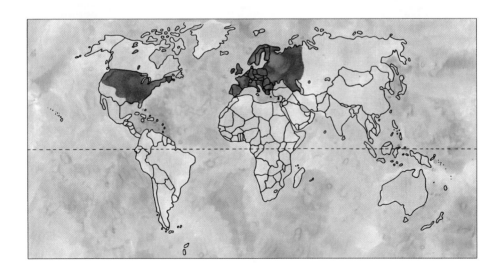

Toxicology

The substance that makes uncooked lorchels dangerous to humans is monomethylhydrazine (MMH), which can damage the central nervous system, the stomach, and the liver.

Symptoms

Symptoms of MMH poisoning begin within 6 to 12 hours of ingestion and include nausea, vomiting, watery diarrhea, abdominal cramps, weakness, headache, muscle cramps (from dehydration), jaundice, rapid pulse, high fever, dizziness, faintness, loss of coordination, and in severe cases, convulsions, coma, and death.

Treatment

Within six hours of ingestion, before vomiting and diarrhea occur, induce vomiting or administer activated charcoal and gastric lavage. Anticonvulsants may be required. Replace fluids to counteract dehydration.

Prevention

• If you are planning to eat lorchels, the safest way to prepare them is to parboil the mushrooms and throw away that first pot of water, then boil them a second time, drain them (again throwing away the water), and then cook them in any manner.

Merely inhaling the fumes from boiling lorchels can lead to severe illness.

A toxin derived from lorchels is an essential ingredient in rocket fuel.

MAGIC MUSHROOM

HOW IT GETS PEOPLE

Species: Psilocybe cubensis

RATING

HABITAT

HABITAT

HABITAT

CLIMATIC ZONE

CLIMATIC ZONE

The magic mushroom is perhaps the most sought–after of the hallucinogenic mushrooms, which, when ingested, produce some startling
changes in one's sensations and perceptions. Europeans first encount-
ered magic mushrooms during the Spanish conquest of the Americas.
Because of the important role the mushrooms played in the religions of

the Native Americans, the Spaniards, and especially the Roman Catholic missionaries among them, suppressed their use to such an extent that the very existence of such mushrooms was called into doubt by later botanists.

Magic mushrooms were not rediscovered by non–Native Americans until the early 20th century, when they were found in Oaxaca, in southern Mexico near the Pacific coast. Eventually, they were identified by botanists as part of the *Psilocybe* genus of mushrooms. Since then, the mushrooms have been fervently hunted by people seeking to experience altered states of reality. Such "recreational" mushroom use peaked in the 1960s and 1970s but still continues to a certain extent today.

Name/Description

The magic mushroom, *Psilocybe cubensis*, is particularly abundant in the Pacific Northwest, where it can usually be found growing on or around

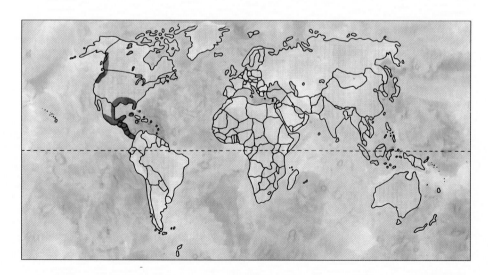

manure in cattle pastures. Magic mushrooms are small, seldom growing taller than four inches, and they are white to pale yellow in color. Their caps are bell–shaped and have a thick, sticky consistency. The stem will turn blue when handled or bruised.

Toxicology

The two primary hallucinogenic substances in magic mushrooms are psilocybin and psilocin.

Symptoms

Symptoms of magic mushroom intoxication resemble those induced by LSD and usually begin within 30 to 60 minutes of ingestion. These symptoms include heightened color perception and other visual distortions and hallucinations, elation, hilarity, delusions, anxiety, paranoia, panic, abnormal muscle movements, dilated pupils, vertigo, lack of coordination, weakness, drowsiness, and, in children, high fever and convulsions. Symptoms usually pass within six hours.

Treatment

In case of accidental ingestion or adverse reaction, the victim should be kept calm and repeatedly assured that the effects of the mushroom are only temporary. If possible, keep the victim in an environment that is familiar and unthreatening. Tranquilizers or sedatives may be helpful if the victim is very agitated. High fever in children should be controlled by sponging with tepid water.

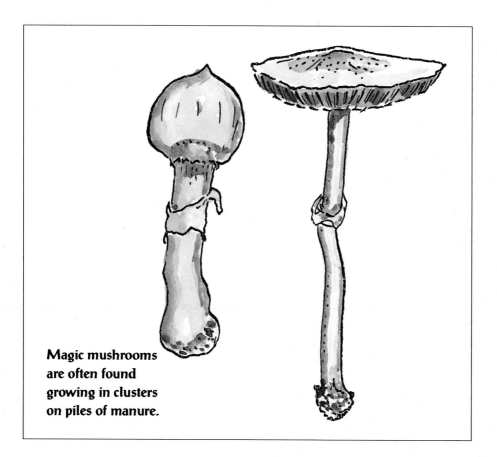

Magic mushrooms
are often found
growing in clusters
on piles of manure.

MANCHINEEL TREE

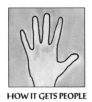

HOW IT GETS PEOPLE

Species: Hippomane
mancinella

HOW IT GETS PEOPLE

HABITAT

CLIMATIC ZONE

RATING

In November 1498, Christopher Columbus, engaged in his second voyage to the New World, anchored his ship off the Island of Marie Galante, a dependency of Guadeloupe. Going ashore, Columbus and his men found a pleasant little tree growing on the beach. The tree bore tempting little fruit that looked like crab apples. The sailors named the tree *manzanillo*, Spanish for "little apple tree." After sampling the "little apples," however, they probably used much harsher language to describe the tree, at least until their mouths and throats had grown so painfully swollen that swearing became difficult.

Manchineel Tree

In Florida, around the Caribbean, and in the West Indies, the toxic manchineel tree continues to this day to bedevil both native inhabitants and visitors alike. And one does not have to taste its apples to get poisoned. On Caribbean beaches, people still seek out the manchineel's cool shade, only to be burned by toxic dew falling from its leaves. Manchineel wood is prized by furniture makers, but carpenters who forget to properly burn the wood before they begin working on it are poisoned by the sap. Even attempts to prevent poisonings sometimes result in poisonings; laborers hired to cut down manchineel trees have been squirted in the eyes with sap—and subsequently blinded—as they hacked at a tree with an ax.

Name/Description

The manchineel tree, *Hippomane mancinella*, can grow to be about 50 feet tall. It has light gray bark; broad, smooth, attractive leaves that provide abundant shade; and little yellow- or rose-colored flowers. The fruit of the manchineel tree resembles crab apples.

Pharmacology

Manchineel extracts have reportedly been used to treat cancer, infections, paralysis, skin disorders, venereal disease, tetanus, and warts.

Toxicology

The principal toxin in manchineel trees is believed to be physostigmine.

Symptoms

The sap of the manchineel tree is extremely caustic. Direct contact with the skin can cause burning of the skin, painful swelling, and pustular eruptions. Contact with the eye can cause severe irritation and temporary—and in some cases permanent—blindness. Smoke from a burning manchineel tree or its parts can cause respiratory irritation, eye inflammation and irritation, and headache. Ingesting manchineel fruit causes swelling and pain in the mouth and throat, inflammation and ulceration of the lining of the stomach and the intestines, vomiting, abdominal pain, bloody diarrhea, and possibly death.

Treatment

For skin poisoning, immediately wash the affected area and apply a soothing lotion with a cortisone derivative. For eye irritation, wash out the eyes with water. Use conjunctivitis eyedrops if necessary. If ingestion occurs, administer gastric lavage. In extreme cases, respiratory assistance may be required.

**Dew from machineel tree leaves is toxic
enough to burn human flesh.**

NUX VOMICA

HOW IT GETS PEOPLE

Genus: Strychnos

HABITAT

CLIMATIC ZONE

RATING

In 31 B.C., the armies of Roman emperor Augustus defeated the combined forces of Queen Cleopatra of Egypt and Roman general Marc Antony at the Battle of Actium. In despair, Marc Antony, who was Cleopatra's lover as well as her ally, committed suicide. Soon after, Cleopatra was captured by Octavian at Alexandria. She decided to follow Marc Antony and began contemplating the method she would use. According to legend, she considered using the poison strychnine, an extract of the nux vomica tree. She obtained some of this substance, summoned one of her slaves, and ordered him to ingest a lethal dose in order to see what kind of death awaited her. A few minutes after taking the poison, the slave began suffering horrific seizures. The convulsions were so violent that his entire body arched and stiffened until only the back of his head and his heels touched the ground. A hideous grimace was frozen on the slave's face. The unfortunate man remained conscious throughout the ordeal, right up until the moment of his death. Cleopatra quickly eliminated strychnine from her list of options. She eventually chose to die by the bite of a poisonous snake.

Name/Description

Nux vomica is a medium-sized evergreen with a maximum height of about 40 feet. It has a crooked, thick trunk and irregular branches covered with smooth, ash-colored bark. Nux vomica leaves are oval in shape, heavily veined, shiny, and smooth to the touch. Clusters of greenish white, funnel-shaped flowers hang from the ends of the branches; they are followed by small, orange-red berries.

Pharmacology

Nineteenth-century physicians generally believed strychnine to be a central nervous system stimulant, and they added small amounts of it to

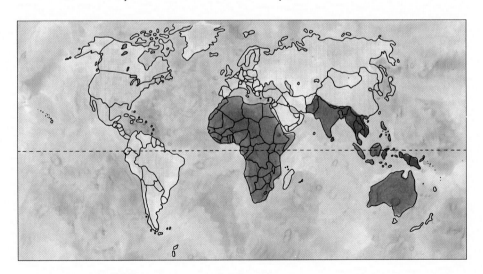

medicinal tonics. Today's physicians use strychnine to stimulate muscular activity, and it is used in certain neurological treatments to stimulate specific nerve centers. Strychnine is also known as an antidote to poisoning from alcohol and other central nervous system depressants.

Toxicology

The entire nux vomica growth, including the seeds, is poisonous. The primary toxin is strychnine.

Symptoms

Symptoms of strychnine poisoning usually appear within 20 minutes of ingestion. Initial symptoms include restlessness, irritability, and anxiety. In cases of severe poisoning, these symptoms will be followed by violent spasmatic convulsions, affecting the entire body and even the face, caused by overstimulation of the spinal nerve tissue, or ganglia. Between convulsions there will be complete muscle relaxation. Further seizures can be brought on by any external stimuli, such as a sudden noise, touch, or bright light. During the convulsions, the victim's blood pressure will rise dramatically and he or she will turn blue in the face. The pulse will be rapid and feeble. Respiratory distress will lead to death.

Treatment

Immediately induce vomiting, and then give copious amounts of very strong black tea to the victim. The tannic acid in the tea will neutralize the strychnine. (Urethane in large doses is also an antidote to strychnine poisoning.) Induce vomiting again, followed by more tea; repeat this process until the victim reaches medical aid. Avoid subjecting the victim to any unnecessary external stimuli.

**Strychnine, the nux vomica plant 's toxin, is
a common ingredient in rat poisons.**

OLEANDER

HOW IT GETS PEOPLE

Species: Nerium oleander

HOW IT GETS PEOPLE

CLIMATIC ZONE

CLIMATIC ZONE

HABITAT

RATING

The port city of Nice, France, is considered one of the most colorful in all of Europe. Its waterfront is lined with buildings washed in charming hues of ochre and pink. Large, fragrant oleander bushes with their abundant clusters of cheerful white, pink, or reddish blossoms add to the color. Oleander can be found in almost every port on the Mediterranean coast; like the palm tree of the tropics, it is a part of the landscape, the perennial delight of tourists, painters (especially watercolorists), and photographers. It is hard to imagine that such a pretty plant is also a killer.

Oleander

During World War I, many French soldiers stationed in Greece died after mistaking oleander for bay leaf and wrapping legs of lamb in oleander leaves before roasting them over open fires. And in the south of France, hungry tourists are still being poisoned after roasting sausages on skewers made from oleander branches. Children, as always, are at greatest risk. In India, numerous children have died from eating the attractive flowers. In Florida recently, a four-year-old developed symptoms of heart failure merely from licking the sticky oleander sap off his fingers. And children and adults alike have been poisoned by spreading their toast with honey gathered from bees that fed on oleander nectar.

Name/Description

Oleander, also known as common oleander, pink oleander, rose bay, and pink laurel, is an ornamental evergreen native to the Mediterranean but now widely cultivated elsewhere. Oleander shrubs usually grow 6 to 9 feet tall, but they have been known to grow to 20 feet in some areas.

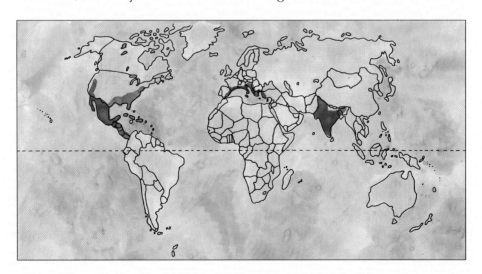

Oleander is characterized by leathery, oblong, sharply pointed leaves of up to 10 inches in length and by clusters of fragrant white, pink, or rosy blossoms.

Toxicology

All parts of the oleander bush are poisonous, especially the seeds. Smoke from burning oleander leaves and water in which oleander flowers has been placed are also highly toxic. The primary toxins in oleander are oleandrin and neriin; their effect on the human heart is similar to that of digitalis (see Foxglove). A single oleander leaf is considered potentially lethal.

Symptoms

Contact with oleander has been known to cause skin irritation and inflammation. In cases of ingestion, symptoms develop quickly. They include inflammation of the lining of the stomach and intestines, vomiting, cardiac irregularities such as a high pulse rate, coldness in the extremities, dizziness, dilation of the pupils, discoloration around the mouth, sweating, bloody feces, abdominal pain, convulsions, respiratory paralysis, unconsciousness, and death. Some victims have also experienced delirium, visual disturbances, and hallucinations.

Treatment

For skin contact, immediately wash the affected area and apply a soothing lotion. For ingestion, induce vomiting or administer gastric lavage. Activated charcoal may be given later to absorb any remaining toxins. Heart-regulating drugs may be required.

Many people have been poisoned by eating honey made from oleander nectar.

Prevention

- Although it is hard to imagine the port towns and cities of the Mediterranean without oleander, in some areas new restrictions against its cultivation are being established, prohibiting the growing of oleander outside screened patios or other protected areas.

POISON HEMLOCK

HOW IT GETS PEOPLE

Species: Conium maculatum

CLIMATIC ZONE

HABITAT

HABITAT

HABITAT

RATING

Poison hemlock extract has a prominent place in the history of poisons. It was at one time the state poison of Athenian Greece. The most famous victim of poison hemlock was the Greek philosopher Socrates. In 399 B.C., Socrates was condemned to death by poisoning for the "crimes" of impiety and corruption of the young people of Athens. The philosopher Plato, who studied under Socrates, was present as the death sentence was carried out. After drinking down the cup of poison hemlock extract,

Poison Hemlock

Socrates, wrote Plato, "walked about until, as he said, his legs began to fail, and then he lay on his back, according to the directions, and the man who gave him the poison now and then looked at his feet and legs; and after a while he pressed his foot hard, and asked him if he could feel; and [Socrates] said, No; and then [the man pressed] his leg, and so upwards and upwards, and showed us that [Socrates' legs were] cold and stiff. And [Socrates] felt [his legs] himself, and said: When the poison reaches the heart, that will be the end. He was beginning to grow cold about the groin, when . . . he said—they were his last words—he said: Crito, I owe a cock to Asclepius; will you remember to pay the debt? The debt shall be paid, said Crito; is there anything else? There was no answer to this question."

Poison hemlock is no longer used as a method of capital punishment, but it does continue to cause deaths, mostly from accidental ingestion. Many unfortunate victims have been poisoned after sprinkling their food with the seeds, mistaking them for anise or caraway seeds. Poison hemlock leaves are frequently mistaken for parsley and added to salads. And other victims have mistaken poison hemlock for wild parsnip, carrots, or artichokes. Errors such as these often prove to be fatal.

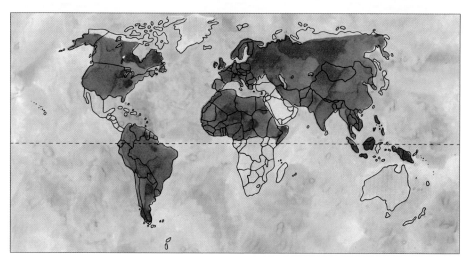

Dangerous Plants and Mushrooms

Name/Description

Poison hemlock, *Conium maculatum*, is a large, coarse, branching herb. A member of the carrot family, poison hemlock is an attractive plant, with lacy, finely divided leaves and flat clusters of white flowers. Poison hemlock has a white root and can grow as tall as eight feet. When crushed, the leaves produce an unpleasant odor.

Toxicology

The entire plant is poisonous, especially the roots and seeds and the leaves during flowering. The primary toxin is coniine, which affects respiratory muscles.

Symptoms

Symptoms of hemlock poisoning include irritation of the mouth and throat, nausea, numbness in the extremities, headache, dilation of the pupils, thirst, sweating, dizziness, weakness, and sometimes convulsions. Death is caused by respiratory paralysis.

Treatment

Administer activated charcoal. Inducing vomiting may be difficult (and dangerous) because of a lockjawlike effect caused by the poison; if this situation develops, administer gastric lavage instead. Artificial respiration may be required.

Poison hemlock is one of the most deadly plants found in the Northern Hemisphere.

POISON IVY

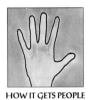

HOW IT GETS PEOPLE

Rhus toxicodendron

HOW IT GETS PEOPLE

HABITAT

HABITAT

HABITAT

HABITAT

HABITAT

HABITAT

CLIMATIC ZONE

RATING

Poison ivy has been called the "nightmare of gardeners, the scourge of hikers, and the curse of campers." It carries an allergenic oil called urushiol, which causes notoriously irritating rashes, inflammations, and blisters on the skin of people who come in contact with it. And urushiol affects not only the skin; it can be inhaled into the lungs with the smoke from burning poison ivy, causing horrendous symptoms. During a 1977 forest fire in California, almost one-third of the fire-fighting force was incapacitated in this manner. William Epstein, a dermatologist and poison ivy expert, believes that poison ivy and its cousin poison oak "are possibly the greatest cause of workman's disability in the nation; each year may bring more than 140,000 cases in the workplace, causing perhaps more than 152,000 lost workdays."

Name/Description

Poison ivy, *Rhus toxicodendron*, is a climbing vine found in most of the United States, Mexico, Central America, Japan, and China. Its leaves appear in groups of three; they are greenish in spring and summer, but they turn a conspicuous and attractive red in the fall and winter. The plant has clusters of pungent, greenish yellow flowers and small white berries that each contain a single seed. The root system is tenacious and extremely hard to remove once it has established itself.

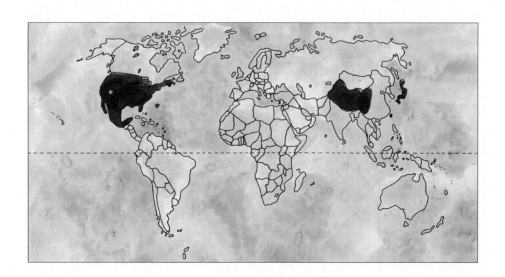

Toxicology

The allergenic oil urushiol is distributed throughout the poison ivy plant and is exuded from breaks in the plant, even if they are so tiny as to be invisible to the human eye.

Animals, clothes, and gardening tools can transmit urushiol, which remains potent for up to a year after leaving the plant.

Symptoms

Symptoms of skin exposure to poison ivy usually develop within a week. Mild exposure will result in itching, burning, and a reddish rash that usually disappears within two weeks. Symptoms of more acute poisoning include intolerable itching and burning and chains of blisters and suppurating sores, which may leave permanent scars. Symptoms of urushiol inhalation include inflammation of the skin over the entire body, fever, severe lung infection, respiratory distress, and death from suffocation if the throat swells shut. Ingestion of poison ivy can also be fatal.

Treatment

Over the centuries, people have gone to great lengths to relieve the torturous itching of poison ivy. They have taken horse–urine baths and cleaned the affected area with everything from gasoline to gunpowder. But no vaccine or cure has yet been found, and treatment must still be given on a symptomatic basis. For skin exposure, wash the affected area immediately after exposure but not after blisters have appeared, as this will only spread the rash. Leave the blisters uncovered. *Do not scratch!* There are many soothing lotions on the market for this situation. For ingestion, induce vomiting. Antacids may relieve subsequent stomach discomfort. Antibiotics may be necessary. For inhalation, treat skin rash

Poison ivy toxin remains viable on clothing contaminated more than a year earlier.

and inflammation as suggested previously. Respiratory infections may require antibiotics. In acute cases, the victim may need respiratory assistance.

Prevention

• If you are planning to enter an area where you know—or even suspect—that there might be poison ivy, cover yourself completely. When gardening, always wear gloves.

SORREL

HOW IT GETS PEOPLE

Species: Rumex acetosa

HOW IT GETS PEOPLE

HABITAT

HABITAT

HABITAT

CLIMATIC ZONE

RATING

The trifoliolate (having three leaflets), jade green, arrow-shaped leaves of the sorrel plant were a regular feature in European vegetable gardens up until the 18th century. Some botanists and herbalists believe that the leaf of the sorrel plant was the one St. Patrick used to symbolize the Holy Trinity to the ancient Irish, although a tiny variety of clover is now generally accepted as the lucky shamrock, or three-leaf clover. High concentrations of oxalic acid and vitamin C give the delicate sorrel leaves a pleasant, vinegar–like taste, and they are frequently used in salads, soups, and sauces. Unfortunately, oxalic acid is toxic as well as tasty. Most victims of sorrel poisoning are livestock that have grazed on raw sorrel, but many people have become sick—and some have died—from eating improperly prepared sorrel leaves. (Sorrel leaves must be boiled, drained, and reboiled in fresh water before they are safe for consumption.) Generally, human fatalities are either the very young or the very old.

Name/Description

Sorrel, *Rumex acetosa*, is native to Europe and Asia but is now well established in North America as well. It is a stout perennial two to three feet tall. The sorrel has a firm stem; in summer, the stem branches into several stalks bearing clusters of small flowers of varying shades of red, green, purple, or brown. (In dry environments, the entire plant may turn brown or red.) Sorrel leaves are extremely sensitive to sunlight and only

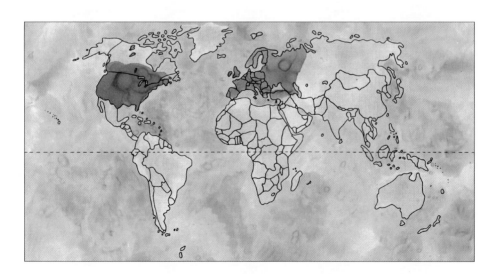

open fully in the shade. If direct sunlight falls on the leaves, they fold together to shield their delicate undersides.

Pharmacology

Because of its high vitamin C content, sorrel was once used as a scurvy preventive. (Scurvy is a debilitating disease caused by vitamin C deficiency. Its most common victims were sailors who could not obtain fresh food on long sea voyages.) Herbalists also recommended sorrel as an appetite stimulant, a diuretic, and an antiseptic, among other things.

Toxicology

The principal toxin in sorrel is oxalic acid.

Symptoms

Symptoms of oxalic acid poisoning include burning and swelling of the mouth, throat, and tongue; impaired speech and breathing, if the swell-ing is extensive; listlessness; loss of muscle control; depression; coma; and occasionally death. Inflammation of the skin may result from external contact with the plant.

Treatment

Induce vomiting. Milk or water may relieve the irritation in the mouth and throat. Otherwise, treat symptomatically.

Despite its toxicity,
sorrel was formerly
used as a diuretic
and an antiseptic.

THE SWEATER

HOW IT GETS PEOPLE

Species: Clitocybe dealbata

HABITAT

CLIMATIC ZONE

RATING

The Sweater? What a strange name for a mushroom! No, the name has nothing to do with the mushroom's appearance. The name *Sweater* refers to the rather strange symptoms caused by ingestion of this mushroom. The Sweater makes you sweat, and sweat profusely. And this is but one of the symptoms of PSL syndrome, or perspiration–salivation–lacrimation syndrome, which is brought on by Sweater ingestion. In severe cases, this trio of symptoms—sweating, drooling, and crying—embarrassing as they may be, is just the beginning.

The Sweater

Name/Description

The Sweater, *Clitocybe dealbata*, is often found in so-called fairy circles of mushrooms, usually in pastures and other grassy areas in the fall. It is common to North America, the British Isles, and Europe. Described as a "drab, undistinguished mushroom," the Sweater has a short, fat stem and a little pointed cap that becomes funnel-shaped as the mushroom ages. Sweaters are grayish or dirty white in color; sometimes they take on a pinkish tinge in damp weather. Young Sweaters have an agreeable odor that is often likened to the smell of freshly cut hay. Older Sweaters smell like bitter almonds.

Toxicology

The principal toxin in the Sweater is muscarine. Small children—especially those with any form of cardiac disease—are extremely susceptible.

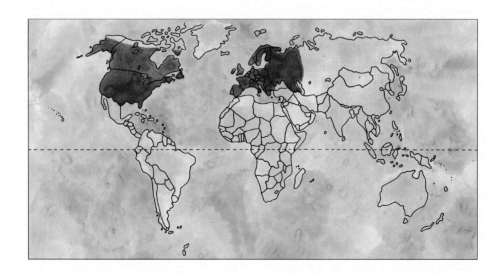

Symptoms

Symptoms of Sweater poisoning appear within two hours of ingestion. Initial symptoms are sudden and excessive perspiration, salivation, and tearing, followed by blurred vision. Vomiting, diarrhea, and painful abdominal cramps will then occur. There may also be constriction of the pupils, falling blood pressure, a slow pulse, labored respiration, and convulsions. Death occurs from cardiac or respiratory failure.

Treatment

Induce vomiting or administer gastric lavage, followed by activated charcoal. Atropine is an antidote to muscarine and should be used in cases of severe poisoning.

Sweater mushrooms remain poisonous
even after thorough cooking.

TOBACCO

HOW IT GETS PEOPLE

Species: Nicotiana tabacum

HOW IT GETS PEOPLE

HABITAT

HABITAT

CLIMATIC ZONE

CLIMATIC ZONE

RATING

The tobacco plant was first brought to Europe from the New World—where it was used by native inhabitants in religious and social ceremonies—at the end of the 16th century. Ironically, the substance that is now recognized worldwide as a major health threat was initially hailed as a cure-all. Called *herba panacea*, or the cure-all herb, it was recommended as a remedy or preventive for all manner of ailments and

106

disorders, including the Black Death, a plague that had devastated Europe during the 14th century. But from the beginning, tobacco had its detractors as well. In a tract entitled "A Counterblast to Tobacco," England's King James I declared that smoking was a "custom lothsome to the eye, hatefull to the Nose, harmeful to the braine, dangerous to the Lungs, and in the blacke stinking fume thereof, neerest resembling the horrible Stigian smoke of the pit that is bottomlesse."

Today, King James's point of view prevails, although nicotine, the powerfully addictive alkaloid in tobacco, is still the most widely abused narcotic in the world. But tobacco can be a threat to the nonaddicted as well, and not only by fouling the air that nonsmokers breathe. Ingestion of tobacco leaves in small amounts can be fatal. Children have been poisoned by sucking on tobacco leaves. And many children have also suffered nicotine poisoning from eating tobacco from cigarettes. Nicotine is in fact so toxic that casual contact with the tobacco plant itself can be dangerous. Laborers on commercial tobacco plantations have been poisoned during harvests from absorbing nicotine through open cuts or sores on their hands and fingers.

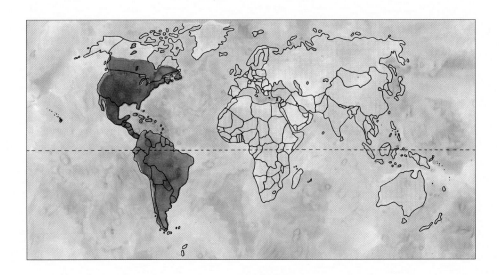

Name/Description

Nicotiana tabacum, the most common form of tobacco, is a tall, erect, annual herb originally native to South America. Growing from 2 to 20 feet tall, the stem and branches bristle with short, sticky hairs and have large, soft, smooth green leaves. Clusters of flowers in shades of green, yellow, or purple grow from the ends of the branches. The flowers open in the evenings or on cloudy days. The fruit of the tobacco plant is a small, oblong capsule containing tiny seeds.

Toxicology

All parts of the tobacco plant, and especially the foliage, contain the extremely toxic alkaloid nicotine, which is absorbed rapidly through the skin, lungs, and mucous membranes.

Symptoms

Symptoms of mild nicotine poisoning are nausea, vomiting, diarrhea, abdominal pains, hand tremors, dizziness, and a slow pulse. If the poisoning is acute, these symptoms will be followed by a shallow and rapid pulse, cold sweats, convulsions, coma, and finally cardiac arrest and possibly death.

Treatment

Wash contaminated skin well with soap and water to prevent or at least reduce the absorption of nicotine. Induce vomiting or administer gastric lavage. Activated charcoal may be given, as well as strong tea. Respiratory assistance and anticonvulsants may be required. Recovery is usually rapid, although there may be residual constipation and urinary retention.

Prevention

• Do not touch, chew, smoke, or sniff tobacco.

Workers harvesting tobacco leaves are frequently poisoned when they absorb nicotine through their skin.

WATER HEMLOCK

HOW IT GETS PEOPLE

Species: Cicuta virosa

CLIMATIC ZONE

HABITAT

HABITAT

RATING

On an early spring morning in Pennsylvania, Chester Mulhollen (age 8), his brother Willard Mulhollen (age 10), and their 9–year–old friend, Harold Fun, came upon some roots in the Mulhollens' yard. Believing the roots to be artichokes, the three boys sat down and had a snack, munching on the roots for about half an hour. A few minutes after they stopped eating, the boys became desperately ill. Chester started toward his house. He reached the door, but then he was stricken with a seizure and collapsed. Despite the efforts of his neighbors and physicians at a local hospital, Chester never regained consciousness. He died later that day. His brother and Harold were luckier; although both suffered the same symptoms as Chester, they survived and recovered.

Water Hemlock

Needless to say, the roots that the three unfortunate boys ate that morning were not artichokes. They were water hemlock roots. As with other poisonous plants, water hemlock's victims are all too often children who mistake it for something else. In some places, water hemlock is known as children's bane. But it is not only the roots of water hemlock that pose a threat. Children have also been poisoned by eating the succulent petioles (a slender stem that supports the blade of a foliage leaf). And children are often tempted to use the hollow stems as whistles or peashooters, a game that usually has an unpleasant ending.

Name/Description

Water hemlock, *Cicuta virosa*, is a poisonous herb of the carrot family. It is also known as spotted cowbane, children's bane, snakeroot, beaver poison, and death–of–man. (In Sweden, water hemlock is known as neckroot, a *neck* being a mysterious little water elf that supposedly feeds on the plant's poisonous roots.) Water hemlock is found in marshy areas in North America, Europe, and Asia. It grows to about six feet and has a

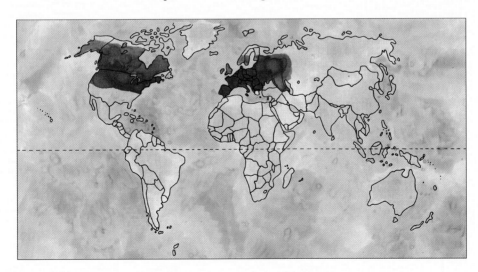

stem with purple spots. When cut or broken, the stem bleeds a yellow, oily sap that smells like parsnips and carrots. Water hemlock roots are tuberous and carrot-shaped and are often partially or completely exposed in marshes. The small white flowers grow in umbrella-shaped clusters.

Toxicology

Water hemlock contains cicutoxin. This poison can be found throughout the entire plant, but it is most heavily concentrated in the roots.

Symptoms

Symptoms of water hemlock poisoning include severe abdominal pain, nausea, vomiting, diarrhea, respiratory distress, excess salivation, tremors, dilated pupils, and delirium. Death is caused by respiratory failure.

Treatment

Induce vomiting or administer gastric lavage. Anticonvulsants and respiratory assistance may be required. Replace lost fluids after vomiting or lavage.

Prevention

• Never eat unidentified wild roots of any kind, no matter what you think they may be.

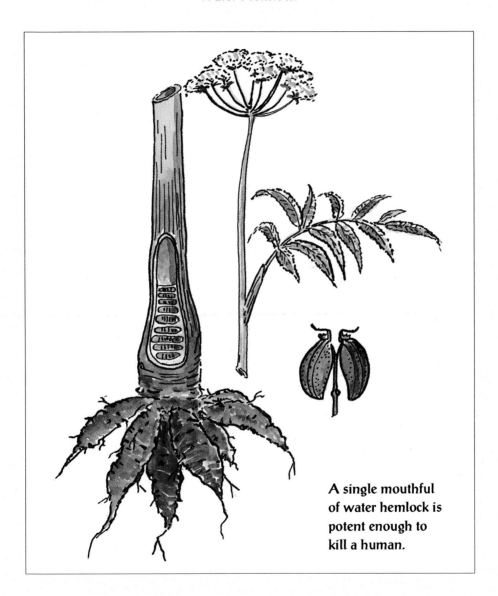

A single mouthful of water hemlock is potent enough to kill a human.

APPENDIX I:
Plant and Mushroom Poisons

A *poison* is defined as a substance that through its chemical action usually kills, injures, or impairs an organism it has entered or come into contact with. The human organism is vulnerable to a wide variety of poisons in the environment. Synthetic poisons are seemingly everywhere; they can be found in household products such as disinfectants, cleaners, hair sprays, cosmetics, paints, and glues; in fumes, gases, and vapors from industrial waste products; and in lawn fertilizers and insect sprays. Most of these synthetic poisons are industrial in origin and are thus relatively new. But *biotoxins*, or naturally produced poisons, were here even before the human race entered the picture.

There are four primary types of biotoxin. Microbial toxins are produced by microscopic organisms, such as bacteria and algae. Zootoxins are the venoms produced by poisonous animals and insects, such as rattlesnakes and hornets. Mushrooms and other fungi produce biotoxins known as mycotoxins. Plant biotoxins are called phytotoxins. (Some plants contain toxins only in certain parts, such as the roots or leaves. The plants and mushrooms discussed in this volume are toxic throughout, although the toxin may be more highly concentrated in one part of the plant or mushroom.) It is thought that biotoxins act primarily as defensive or protective agents, helping mushroom and plant species to survive and prosper.

Mycotoxins and phytotoxins can be just as dangerous as synthetic poisons or animal venoms. They can also be extremely helpful. A large dose of a certain mycotoxin or phytotoxin might have a deadly effect on the human heart, whereas a smaller dose of the same substance might prove to be beneficial to a diseased heart. People have been aware of these properties and have been using these substances to kill or to cure one another since the dawn of civilization, and thus the study and classification of plant and mushroom poisons is an age–old discipline.

Appendix I

In the 1st century A.D., the Greek physician Dioscorides wrote *De materia medica*, the first encyclopedic work on medicinal botany. In the early 11th century, the Persian physician and philosopher Avicenna compiled his *Canon of Medicine*, which for centuries remained the standard reference volume on biotoxins and their antidotes. In the meantime, various practitioners of traditional or folk medicine from cultures around the world continued to collect and pass on information regarding botanical poisons and cures; much of this data was eventually incorporated into the mainstream of medical research and practice. During the 19th and 20th centuries, a vast wealth of new information concerning plant and mushroom poisons and their effects—both positive and negative—has been gathered and put to use, although our knowledge and understanding of the subject is by no means complete. Indeed, many modern botanists feel that the curative potential of plants and mushrooms has only just begun to be realized. It is conceivable that somewhere deep in the South American jungles or in some shadowy forest of the Pacific Northwest, an unlovely mushroom or a blossoming flower holds the secret to curing cancer or one of the other ailments that currently plague humankind.

APPENDIX II:
Shock

Shock, a term that many people use informally, is in medical terms a profoundly disturbing, often fatal condition characterized by a failure of the circulatory system to maintain an adequate blood supply to vital organs. It can be caused by severe injury, blood loss, or disease.

Shock is a state in which perfusion (passage of blood to the vessels) and the blood flow to peripheral tissues are inadequate to sustain life because of insufficient levels of carbon dioxide in the blood or maldistribution of blood flow. Shock is associated with diminished peripheral circulation, hypotension (abnormally low blood pressure), and oliguria (diminished urine output).

Other symptoms are lethargy, confusion, and somnolence (unnatural drowsiness). The victim's hands and feet are cold, moist, and often cyanotic (having a bluish discoloration as a result of insufficient oxygen in the blood), and his or her pulse is weak and rapid.

Untreated, shock is usually fatal. Treatment depends on the cause, the presence of a preexisting or complicating illness, and the time between onset and diagnosis. The victim should be kept warm, with legs raised slightly to improve circulation. The victim's airway and ventilation should be checked, and respiratory assistance should be given if necessary. The head of a shock victim should be turned to one side to prevent choking on his or her own vomit.

FURTHER READING

Arora, David. *Mushrooms Demystified.* Berkeley, CA: Ten Speed Press, 1986.

Eshleman, Alan. *Poison Plants.* Boston: Houghton Mifflin, 1977.

Frohne, Dietrich, Pfander Frohne, and Hans Jurgen. *A Color Atlas of Poisonous Plants.* London: Wolfe Publishing, 1983.

Furst, Peter. *Mushrooms.* New York: Chelsea House, 1986.

Lange, Morten, and Bayard Hora. *Collins Guide to Mushrooms & Toadstools.* London: Collins, 1975.

Lincoff, Gary, and D. H. Mitchel. *Toxic and Hallucinogenic Mushroom Poisoning.* New York: Van Nostrand Reinhold, 1977.

Morton, Julia F. *Exotic Plants.* New York: Golden Press, 1971.

Richardson, Joan. *Wild Edible Plants.* Freeport, ME: DeLorme, 1981.

Richardson, P. Mick. *Flowering Plants.* New York: Chelsea House, 1986.

INDEX

Index

Missy Allen is a writer and photographer whose work has appeared in *Time, Geo, Vogue, Paris-Match, Elle,* and many European publications. Allen holds a master's degree in education from Boston University. Before her marriage to Michel Peissel, she worked for the Harvard School of Public Health and was director of admissions at Harvard's Graduate School of Arts and Sciences.

Michel Peissel is an anthropologist, explorer, inventor, and author. He has studied at the Harvard School of Business, Oxford University, and the Sorbonne. Called "the last true adventurer of the 20th century," Peissel discovered 14 Mayan sites in the eastern Yucatán at the age of 21 and was the youngest member ever elected to the New York Explorers Club. He is also one of the world's foremost experts on the Himalayas, where he has led 14 major expeditions. Peissel has written 14 books, which have been published in 83 editions in 15 countries.

When not found in their fisherman's house in Cadaqués, Spain, with their two young children, Peissel and Allen can be found trekking across the Himalayas or traveling in Central America.

ACKNOWLEDGMENTS

The authors would like to thank Lisa Bateman for her editorial assistance; Brian Rankin for his careful typing; Carla Maristany for her graphic designs; and Linnie Greason, Heather Moulton, and Luis Abiega for so kindly allowing their lives to be infiltrated by these creepy crawlies and ferocious fauna.

CREDITS

All the original watercolor illustrations are by Michel Peissel. The geographic distribution maps are by Diana Blume.